Must a Violence

KUHL HOUSE POETS

edited by Mark Levine

Must a Violence

Poems by

ONI BUCHANAN

UNIVERSITY OF IOWA PRESS

Iowa City

University of Iowa Press, Iowa City 52242
Copyright © 2012 by Oni Buchanan
www.uiowapress.org
Printed in the United States of America

Design by Barbara Haines

The University of Iowa Press is a member of Green Press Initiative and is committed to preserving natural resources.

Printed on acid-free paper

LCCN: 2012932829
ISBN-13: 978-1-60938-129-5
ISBN-10: 1-60938-129-7

for Nibbles and Sergei

Kopper, Kishacoquillas, and Buttons

CONTENTS

IV.

V.

I.

Then From Our Green Branch

then the "safety net" they held

under a branch

then they hit the branch

with a stick

and all of us who weren't holding

tight right at that

second, or if we

forgot, or

we lifted a foot to say, or

a foot to launch, or go, or

if dozing, if we'd been

looking upward through leaves

at a shifting

polygon of sky, or if from the beating we

lost our sense

if we got

dizzy couldn't hold if

the quaking

scared some youngers

or the ground below loomed

in seasick waves, then from our

green branch

we were shaken

dislodged, we

fell from our green canopy

into something

colder—

No Blue Morpho

I wanted
the Blue Morpho
to anoint me
with his fragility
I was in his presence
in the tent
of butterflies
he did not land
on me though I stood
very still for a long
time very still
with my arm
extended like a thin
resilient branch
buoyant curious respectful
a pliant limb I thought
venturing into the scented air
of blossoms and delicate
curling offshoots
a graceful arc of tender
branch but he did not
land on me I tried
to look succulent I
imagined myself
exuding fragrance
and the lobes of my ears

ripened taut with
the redolent essence
of honeysuckle
but no Blue Morpho
came to alight upon
my shoulder and unfurl
his slender tongue
toward the delicate
curve the rosy curve
no Blue Morpho
alighted upon me
that day beneath
the butterfly canopy
the air was
mixed part saturated
warmth fertile humidity
part the cries of a caged
canary part the effervescent
sound of evaporating
mist from the cascades
of a man-made waterfall
I stood very still hoping
to be mistaken
for something more
beautiful more luxuriant
luminous tropical a fragrant
possibility but no
Blue Morpho anointed me
with his delicate foot

no Blue Morpho landed
momentarily on my
outstretched arm to
breathe his shimmery
wings and launch
again no Blue
Morpho drew a curve
in air that rested
on my shoulder for
a solitary point
instead in my
perfect concentrated
stillness I heard
for the first
time the microtones
of wing scales drifting
softly and invisibly
through the heated air
microscopic motes of
color-fashioned dust
descending through the
perfumed air
as various butterflies
brushed imperceptibly by
the scales
accidentally sounding
as they fell the
air itself brushed
their sound I

overheard that nearly
imperceptible symphonic
grid that map of tones
within the satiated air
that net of sounds
that caught me in its
webbing that fell
from wingtips delicacies
dropped by the
Blue Morpho as he
flew on in unerring
loops his joy
beamed elsewhere
nonintersecting beacon

When All the Leaves

When all the leaves fell

the wasp nest hung in its gray paper,
bobbing in the empty air

When all the autumn leaves fell

it was like the trees pitched their trash
on the ground; the trees
trashed everything

When all the colored leaves fell off their branches

I saw a man
hobbling through the changing piles of leaves.
The wind accumulated some
then re-mixed the leaves;
the colors a re-mix

When the leaves fell singly down

each leaf lay face-down on the sidewalk
and left its final exhale there. Each leaf
left a leaf-print, it left a chalk outline,
signature: I was here, Leaf

When the leaves all fell at once

I saw a rat in the mid-afternoon. He stood shaking

on the open lawn. His whiskers trembled and his body
trembled. What's happening to me, ideal
blue day, patch of sunlight on the lawn stuck
with fallen leaves—

A rusted boat hull overturned by the dock

Canada geese nipping up the frayed ends of drying grasses

Bells that carry farther in the air

A tarnished wedding ring bought at a street carnival

When the leaves piled on the ground

plastic bags blew like banners
in the bare, black branches, waylaid
insignia

When the leaves got puked onto the ground

I saw a beer bottle wedged hard
onto a branch.
I saw a bumblebee nearly motionless
on a blasted marigold. He was
waiting for some fold to overtake the stilled
glass windows of his wings—Here I will rest—

A rabbit who was once nearby that fire bush

A rabbit who once leapt down the hillside as I approached

A rabbit who once, nearly invisible in the shadow of that sculpted topiary—

A tiny rabbit once at the edge of the underbrush

A tiny rabbit who once pulled down a stem of grass taller than himself

All the invisible rabbits are there now

where once a rabbit was

The Cheshire Cat

A visitor had abandoned his heavy luggage
in the corner of my bedroom, leather suitcases
unbuckled and various garments spilling out.
Alone in my diaphanous and ruffled nightgown,
I sauntered over to examine
the strewn pile of clothes and bags, the wreckage,
when I saw a small, furry trembling thing, a creature
looking up at me
from an incomprehensible knot of shirts.
I held out my hands and it
leapt into my cupped palms, a tiny
Cheshire cat! "A Cheshire cat!" I thought.
"I've never seen a real one!
If it bites me, that's extremely
good luck," I remembered. I looked
at the Cheshire cat. A huge smile
had spread all the way across its
tiny face. It had beautiful white
pointy teeth, perfectly aligned.
It looked at me like it loved me most
in all the world. It glanced at my
bare white forearm exposed beneath
a sleeve frill of my gown. It looked up at me
again and its smile spread even

wider, then it turned and executed an
enormous chomp into my bare
arm. "It bit me!!" I thought, wild with
joy and disbelief. "This will be
the luckiest year of my life!"

An Infection

An infection had crept in
beneath the dermis and spread
subcutaneously clinging

to the underside of the skin.
The underside of the skin
was the ceiling of the infection.

The infection may have come from
too much scratching of the open wound,
too much scratching of the sores

clotted on the scalp.
The infection may have come
because the hot and crowded train

did not have properly fresh
head napkins on its seats.
The infection may have come at the

International Terminal while waiting
with an empty wheelchair, sitting
in an empty wheelchair to pass the time.

*

The selection at the lunch truck
is not what you'd call extensive.

If only everyone could just take care

of themselves and take cover from the
wetness and rotting. If only everyone
had the common sense and decency

to find a shelter within their means
and then keep the shelter clean and tidy.
A poll was taken

at the public library, the designated
polling place of our precinct.
But no officers dared hand out

in person the summonses to jury duty;
these they sent anonymously
in the mail.

*

The lunch truck
offered a special minestrone soup
on Tuesdays and a giant cookie

baked in the bowels
of the truck. A person could lose himself
if he didn't take care

if he willfully
compromised his boundaries if he
scratched and scratched

on a train crowded
with sweat-drenched passengers. He
touched the seats and chewed on his

fingernails. He pushed the dirty
public wheelchair
of the self-appointed invalid.

Chocolate mist rose
from the truck's bowels,
enshrouded its workers.

December 24

The sirens are wailing down Washington Street.
Down Washington Street the bunched cars part to either curb.

In the square's center, an immense pine tree stands
strung with lights by the bank placard.

Waiting, we read the digits of time, the digits of temperature.
The wind's fingers worm through the stitches of our scarves.

No clothes fasten close enough that the wind cannot undo.
The glass day leans blue against the tall facades.

Here at the bus stop, a measly hoard of individuals waits
to be transported by the number 86.

If it comes, we will file on, orderly, rustling coats and bags.
The shabby bags look beaten on the sidewalk.

If it comes, we will ride down Market Street away,
soaring in our rigid plastic seats.

The only real birds that come here anymore are cardinals
beating the hoards of English sparrows back.

Just before I took the outside stairs, I saw one
fly into a bush of dead brown branches.

I held my breath and watched its red flickering,
a fluttering heart inside the brittle, leafless volume of the bush.

Its redness turned over and over inside the dead brown
like an exquisite gem in a mud-caked palm.

A pulsing of red like the beat in a sweeping lighthouse beacon
where it meets and meets again a still observer's eye.

I watched the quick flash of its vivid red,
the angular skittish turns inside the dead

remnants of sticks. And pulled myself away for what?
For what.

A Long Blue Distance

The designated "Military Area" had no
structure anywhere in sight, just an exit ramp
leading off the main road and
disappearing entirely into a curve
of scorched hillside.

I drove down the mountain into parched
barren land—burnt brown hills
with some sprinkling of overcooked green,
the hills folding and crumpling,
full of creases.

Occasional grazing cattle
chewed what seemed like sticks
and long brown shoots of hollow stalks.

When I stopped and stepped into the air,
I saw a lumber mill across the street.
Horizontal green pipes up on high stilts
traversed from one green warehouse
to another, dreaming up above the ground—

The sun was frigid in the mountains!

I was told the town used to have its own
mountain goat which could be seen
on some narrow ledge or other
on a certain cliff face between exits 7B and 6.

Back on the blurred highway, I missed
my exit and took instead a road that led
through a shimmering grove, all the trees
waving their golden fans against the bright blue sky,
teasing and swaying.

How evenly they were planted—
in avenues and alleys—I could look
a long blue distance into the grove
and driving by, the lanes of sky
rotated into view then spun away
like spokes—

"He Who Roams the Plains"

Mtembei, the youngest giraffe

I am the dream of the Serengeti
as its drowsy gold expanse
dozes under cloud shadows.

As the spotted surface of the sleeping field,
I lift away, am sewn together in the breeze—
a tall dream filled with length and hay.

But, living now, having come
into this world, having filled
a body, an epic journey

across dusty folds of hot dry land,
migration inland to a secret
source of water—what am I now?

The sudden showers dampen down
my horns. I hear distant rhythms
in the swaying grasses. The airborne seeds

drift by on wands of wind
like missives from that former
hovering world. My hooves clack

on the sun-baked mud. Here.
Here. And mirrored
in the watering hole.

All the inaccessible
highest branches flaunt
their full green leaves, the

shapely edges winking to me, twinkling—
I'm hoisting myself high, higher to see—
But I am only a baby. How will I

know the moment? Will it be an aperture
of light growing wider, growing brighter, or
a far-flung colored beam? Will I see

a radiant face among the throngs,
a gaze that turns toward me and
connects and locks

into my long-lashed
eyes? Will I overhear a shred of melody,
an ancient song I recognize?

If You Love an Animal

I'm making myself cry.
I'm looking at myself in the mirror crying, which makes me cry.
"Look, I'm crying," I sob.
But no one hears me.
No one. Because I'm deserted and neglected and alone.
And my face is dirty.
I'm a tear-stained orphan and my last meal was bark from a tree.

"If you're taking care of an animal, be careful
not to drop that animal," I said aloud, people coming and going
and that little animal in its cage on its soiled cedar chips,
shifting its cedar chips from one side of the cage to the other,
"if you're going to take care of an animal, remember
to pick up that animal every day and not
to drop it," I advised, "be careful to support that animal
as you lift it into the air, to make it feel safe, it is
leaving the ground unexpectedly and without its
choice necessarily, it is important
to handle an animal properly."

Before I get too overcome with my ability
to enjoy the sunny day, I'm going to have to re-read
my diary and also think about
injustice.
I'm going to need to conceal my diary beneath my

ragged garments and transport it
into the forest where I will build
a lean-to of sticks and call it my home.
This is where I live now, here with the ferns
that bend and sway. I pulled a tire out of the stream
and dragged it back to my fire pit, putrid filth
spilling out from inside as the wheel rolled.
A stripe of stench across my face like war paint.
I hammered a nail into a tree.
I shall hang my coat here
as I clear the brush from my meager shelter.
I live in the forest. The animals
understand me and the leaves make gentle crunching sounds
underfoot and the bare branches make patterns in the sky.

"If you're taking care of an animal, clip its nails
very carefully so you don't get too close
to the quick," I instructed, "you want to get
close enough to the quick that the animal
can leap and run with no discomfort at all, you see
an animal really should not know
about its nails, that its nails might be a problem, an animal
should not experience even a
vague awareness that its nails might be
holding it back," I went on,
"in the wild, an animal would wear down
its nails naturally, with all its goings-on
upon the rock-strewn ground
in the landscape of boulders and moss, with its

scratching of tunnels from dirt or
scratching of insects from bark,
in the forest an animal
would keep its nails trim without even trying,
its nails would take care
of themselves as a natural by-product
of self-sufficiency, a reward of survival."

I'm bleeding onto some sheets of newsprint
to record the drama of my bleeding.
My nose is gushing blood but I refuse to
pinch the bridge. I insist
on bleeding freely. No one can stop
me. I live in the moment.
I am an orphan crouched in a corner
eating a crust of bread off a broken piece of tile.
I bleed over the pages of the Daily News blown toward me.
When the pages dry, I will seal them in envelopes
addressed to my pen pals. I've never met my pen pal in Sweden
but her name is Angela Petrov.
I have a pen pal in Egypt named Tamer El Said,
one in Greece named Isil Miritzi,
and one in Phoenix, Arizona, a girl
who was my friend before she moved away.

"If you love an animal, why would you leave it
alone in its tiny cage with all its waste,
it's doing its best to keep itself clean, but there's only so much

a small domestic animal can control about its habitat,"
I hissed this with a hint of accusation,
"why do you let your animal chew away
a patch of its own fur, turning and chewing and chewing,
and the bottoms of its feet
raw with sores from the wire mesh,
you say so many things
but if you love an animal, you should give it
fresh water and a food dish that
doesn't flip up into its face
when it tries to eat its pellets,
pellets are not an animal's favorite food
anyway," I revealed, "and
if you think you own
an animal, then why not buy, since you can,
that animal's friend, why not
also own that animal's friend, not everything
should have to be so hard and lonesome
for an animal in your care."

My ponytail is yanked and disheveled.
My tears run down over the red welt the shape
of a hand print. I have to count the friendship pins
that I keep in a cream cheese tub in my top
dresser drawer. I want to write all my pen pals while
the sun comes in at the window, shining right through
the yellow curtains, through my mobile
of folded paper birds. I want to crack
all the codes in the back of the Code Book

and win the Grand Prize which I already know
will be working as a spy for the government.
I want to make a rainbow-colored bracelet
out of embroidery floss and knots. I want to tally
the cereal box UPC symbols I'm saving
and wind up the music box that plays *Swan Lake*
and cry and cry as the toothed spool spins around.

"If you love an animal, you must not let it slump
in the heat, you must not leave it in the oppressive heat
to slump and die," I muttered under my breath,
"you must plug in two electric fans
nearby to the animal and train one in a line
perpendicular to the cage, like a peripheral air, like a song
an animal almost remembers, like a friend
an animal remembers, the smell of a friend,
or the way that friend comes close, the approach
of that friend, one fan perpendicular to the cage
like a memory— And the other fan
trained lightly on the cage, but only in a certain area,
so there is a choice, so there's a choice to get shelter
or rest in the gentle, steady wind," I lectured, unsure,
"because the air needs to circulate," I emphasized,
"unless your love is crippled, don't let an animal
cry and cry in the stagnated air,
its breathing tight and difficult,
unless your love is crippled, give an animal
a large environment where it can exercise in
the spaciousness of varied terrain, welcome an animal

into your daily household activities, make
an animal feel included, it's an essential member
of the family, you want an animal to feel
its life is worth something," I soliloquized, "you want an animal
to believe it can contribute happiness, you want
an animal to be free in its expression of itself, you want
it to be free to leap if it leaps or to run if it runs, you don't want an animal
to flinch or panic, you don't want an animal to scurry
into its cedar hut when it sees you coming, you don't want
an animal to cower or scramble, you want an animal to be
free and easy, eager and sincere, you want an animal
to strive and explore and dare
to be its best self," I offered, "an animal wants
to please you, an animal wants to live
in your circle of light, unless your light
is crippled, unless your love is crippled."

II.

Chant of the Killing Jar

after a Navajo crop-harvesting chant ca. 1794, "Songs in the Garden of the House God"

What's that iridescence in the Killing Jar?

What's that buzzing in the Killing Jar?

    Is it you buzzing?

    Is it me buzzing?

    Is it you? Is it me?

What's that enchantment of stained

glasswork in the Killing Jar?

Somebody hand me the Killing Jar.

Which team member hands the Killing Jar?

    Do you hand the Killing Jar?

    Do I hand the Killing Jar?

    Do you hand it? Do I hand it?

    Do you? Do I?

I thought you were carrying the Killing Jar.
If this backpack bears the Killing Jar . . .

I thought I was carrying the Killing Jar.
If this weight is not the Killing Jar . . .

Is it struggling in the Killing Jar?

Is it subsiding in the Killing Jar?

Is there minimal damage to the specimen in the Killing Jar?

How long till it is overcome by

breathing in the Killing Jar?

The tightness of the chest inside the Killing Jar.

The chilling temperature inside the Killing Jar.

The overwhelming fumes inside the Killing Jar.

The spiracles saturated in the Killing Jar.

Is it fully saturated in the Killing Jar?

Is it done now in the Killing Jar?

Did you leave the Killing Jar beneath the ferns?
I was on my hands and knees

Did you leave the Killing Jar at the mouth of the tunnel?
The pathway networked underground

Did you wedge the Killing Jar in that crook?
The roughness of the bark kept it fixed in place

Did you forget the Killing Jar on that flat rock?
Only the visible portion of the rock is known to us

My callouses are rusty from the Killing Jar.

Can we empty out the Killing Jar? I can barely

hold on—somebody unscrew the lid—somebody

help me stuff it in the Killing Jar.

Shall you stuff it in the Killing Jar?

Shall I stuff it in the Killing Jar?

Shall you stuff it in?

Shall I stuff it in?

Shall you? Shall I?

Tactical Subordinates

Tactical Subordinates
Valuable Subordinates
Foreign Subordinates
Alleged Subordinates
Circumstantial Subordinates
Subordinate Behavior
Agreeable Subordinates
Competitive Subordinates
Unscrupulous Subordinates
Provincial Subordinates
Hardy Subordinates
Subordinate Occupation
Ardent Subordinates
Subordinate Realism
Subordinate Growth
Gentle Subordinates
Alert Subordinates
Subordinate Legislation
Reckless Subordinates
Subordinate Cognition
Civil Subordinates
Noble Subordinates
Cunning Subordinates
Implicit Subordinates
Rebellious Subordinates
Encouraging Subordinates
Subordinate Functionality

Steadfast Subordinates

Stable Subordinates

Decent Subordinates

Helpful Subordinates

Subordinate Security

Remote Subordinates

Astute Subordinates

Subordinate Assembly

Subordinate Properties

Scheming Subordinates

Regulated Subordinates

Uniformed Subordinates

Subordinate Ideology

Eager Subordinates

Relations between Subordinates

Defunct Subordinates

Manages Subordinates

Subordinate Protection

Preservation of Subordinates

Insolvency of Subordinates

Subordinate Solution

Subordinate Reputation

Jocular with Subordinates

Hilarity among Subordinates

Subordinate Benefits

Profit from Subordinates

Envy of Subordinates

Subordinate Reconciliation

Harmony among Subordinates

Subordinate Arbitration
Subordinate Esteem
Briefing Subordinates
Backbiting Subordinates
Upbraid Subordinates
Diligent Subordinates
Operational Subordinates
Goodwill among Subordinates
Subordinate Adaptation
Subordinate Identification
Subordinate Implication
Monitoring Subordinates
Integrating Subordinates
Promising Subordinates
Enabling Subordinates
Incentives for Subordinates

Don't Fall, Baba

Don't fall, Baba. It's hard
being a mom, isn't it. I read somewhere
the tragedy of being a mom
is that your child will never love you
as much as you love your child—is that
true, Baba? I don't want you to fall.
When you get hurt, Baba, it makes me
feel physically ill that you were
in any pain at all. I become nauseous
and faint to think of you bleeding
or bruising or breaking a bone.
Baba, take care not to fall!
The buttermilk is in the fridge
and the Rummikub lies dark
in his dark box. His mouth smiles
but his eyes are cold and mean.
He undoes all the rhymes we make.
He scrambles the hard tiles.
Baba, don't fall! The grasshoppers
part to either side in the field,
like the earth unbuttoning, but Baba,
don't go into the earth yet. It's like
you're in another world already, gone
from this place and these spring flowers.
Baba, don't fall. You gave me
a beautiful piece of stationery

to write on. I'm wearing my sundress
and my bathing suit underneath—is it
time for a swim? Can we water
the seedling trees? And race snails
out of a chalk-drawn circle?
The river is running down at the bottom
of the hill, down in the scrubby woods.
I dreamt a terrible thing down there, Baba.
I dreamt my own death up
till I frantic ran by myself through the trees
and ripped my dress on the barbed wire fence,
ducking under to get away from myself.
I have a scar on my back from the barb.
Baba, take me with you again. We can
sing hymns in the white, roadside church.
We can paint birches on a canvas. We can
pull strings from the string beans in the basket.
We can swing in the hammock. We can set up
the wickets and get out the mallets—I don't
want you to fall, Baba—Baba, don't fall!

I Heard Her Long Hair Making Five Sounds

I heard the sound of a bolt of her hair
as she brushed a broad wave of it
away from the left side of her face and
over her shoulder—I heard it lift
into the air and subside again, a brief kite,
or a sail for the body

I heard the sound of her long hair dividing
over her right shoulder as it fell. Some of the hair
fell over the slope of her shoulder to the front, some
fell to the back, and there was a creaking,
the tiniest sound of division
in that rift where the hair fell one way or
fell the other

I heard the sound of her hair
as its length brushed against the knot
of her white cotton sun-shirt where
she had tied it back against her neck:
a hushing sound to soothe
the starched stubbornness, assuaging,
persuading, beguiling, assigning itself
around the contours of the knot, a hushing to make
space in the air

Then the sound of the tips of her hair
as they reached down like the thinnest limp ends

of willow branches to brush against
her denim jeans, the roughness
of the jeans like an injury
to the fine ends of hair that
chafed themselves relentlessly
against it

The length of her hair itself began to sound, or I
began to hear its presence underneath, sounding
as the strings of an instrument
would sound if they were left strung aloft
in a wide field, or hung in a desert, left
to be blown on, or over, blown through
by a passing wind
The length had been making its own sound all the while,
a drone, a constant rising chord,
and the lustre of her hair
gave tone color
to the sound the length made

Five Tiny Doves

It was clear she had carefully considered
which jagged rock

from the pile of rocks provided
for the purpose. Her pitching arm was

winding up. I glanced aside
and saw a school of silvery fish

bank left and right around some
monolithic coral growth, around

a sunken hull of ship. The silver
parted and merged again like

balls of mercury. The hull
was overgrown with waving plants

and strands of ramifying green.
She lashed the whipcord for

more optimal momentum.
I turned my drooping eye and caught

a glimpse of a sea horse disappearing
into dark. The ridges of its

body glistened with mysterious
gems, then another sea horse

propelled into view using its extravagant
dragon-tail. It beckoned me

to follow. How can sunlight
make it down so deep, I thought.

I was concentrating hard.
In the periphery, I saw

the shovel blade bear down
as if upon another's head, hitting

another person. Far up, away,
bared teeth with a distant

blue sky behind— I myself
heard from the bottom of the sea

the folding of an ocean wave
upon its surface, the muted cry

of wheeling seagulls up above,
scavenging and rowdy, somewhere

far out above the blue expanse,
breathing air, occasionally

dipping in. But sound in water— Water,
the conduit of sound! From my ear's

positioning far below the choppy surface,
from my auditory nerves, I heard

inside a saturated seashell's whorl, I heard
the flank of a fish creak

to change its angle, heard acceleration
as it sped away,

the pointillistic gleam
of fluctuating scales.

I heard the effort of a sea slug,
a squeaking on the coral.

I heard a crab dance by on pointed feet
beneath an old crab line

where at the floating end, I heard fraying
of the fibers— Loosen— Slacken into

dark. The lightless bottom, where no
distilled ray will ever penetrate. Oh, the sound

inside the pitch! Nearby, on the darkened
ocean floor, I heard a living sand dollar

drag its mass across the thickening granules.
I heard its velvet spines, its follicles unfurl,

extend and grasp, its cilia grip individual
grains of sand, the rough-cut

edges of the grains, and heave its cumbrous
body forward, overtaking

discarded skeletons and shells
along the way. A living sand dollar

on its path across the sediment! Five tiny doves
live inside that sand dollar—

How much more can I ignore?
I listened for the doves—

Palais de Mari

It is as much   what can be heard   through it as it is

    its own notated   tones: concentrated globes

        like colored droplets sinking   through a viscous

sky, the droplets dilute   themselves with the   volume around them, some

    steadily descend, some   hover and ramify (bleed)

      at different submerged   depths, glass bulbs in

a Galileo thermometer   measuring the temperature   of sonority, the temperature

    of texture, of touch,   the temperature of the effort

      each sound makes, one   to the next, to stretch,

create a line, and of the time   each sound has   left to its body as the decay

    rises from each   nucleus of sound in

      swaths (auras) (stains)   which intersect and mingle with other

swaths, the disintegration, the   decomposition rising off—   The sounds are so soft, the ear

    goes through them to the   instrument itself, the

      mechanical catch of the   single key depressed, partitioning its depth, descent, and the skin   of the key now a layer   apart from the rest of the key, a

surface, epidermis,   the skin of the key an

identity, a friction against   the skin of the finger

whose touch weighs   the lever down, there is blood   underneath the skin, barely,

barely, the   slow hammer rising

inside the black body, almost   negligible, the scent of

metal on the struck string,   the cloud of metallic molecules   puffing off from the

surface of the coiled   wire, an explosion at this level

of magnification, shrapnel   dispersing in

the air in which I   breathe my mind   has never been so

quiet and at the same   time so alert everything

transparent my   skin is growing new cells

I hear their borders   pressing up against   the borders of the current

cells, the blood is   circulating with a low

rumbling, like ribbons drawn   through a cardboard box, once

I made a network of   folded paper channels   in a shoebox

then taped the lid back on,   cut two

holes, you dropped a marble in   the hole in the top

then just listened to it   rolling around inside   the shoebox, traversing

    invisibly the elaborate   inner contours, the idea was

      how long can you keep   the marble moving around

in such a finite space, how   slowly can it traverse   its course, at first I thought

    "how long can you delay   the end," I found

      the second hole, I looked   directly in, I stared without

blinking at that cusp   just inside the box where the   outside light penetrated

    in and was engulfed   by the inside dark, I knew

      if I looked carefully   enough if I held

my breath if I didn't allow   distraction I would   see the marble when it

    emerged from the dark   toward the light now just

      at the brink of light now   at the lip of the hole, crossing

the threshold, out entirely,   falling, the game   is over, the marble

    took x number   of seconds to run its

      course, I stared hard   in the second hole, my eyes

dried out, I   hallucinated multiple   marbles emerging from the

    dark, I thought,   how many deaths

      can befall one witness   searching for death, this is just a game, I thought,   the marble came out   in x number of seconds,

    I dropped the marble   in again, how much

      can you elasticize   the present, how eternal

can you make   the present   moment, there is no

    point just breath   in the body I

    put my ear to the box—

Selection

—   for the   Real   Animals,   the coded
animals   with   their finite   sequences,
live   in a   physical   space
surrounded by   all the   versions   they could
have   been,   the   invisible, the
Almost   Animals,   almost   given
breath   to exist—   or   breath
in time—   just   as breath   sculpted
in time   makes   a rhythm   of real
words   that   fill   portions of
the invisible   grid of   stressed   and unstressed
syllables,   all the   infinite   words
that could   have been   spoken,   sounded
in space.   The grid   extends   in the air,
unfolding   back   through   centuries,
back before   the first   words   were hung
upon it,   ornaments   of proof   and
stretching   onward,   beyond   the languages
we   recognize,   far beyond   our own
scattered   patches   where   on the
tapestry   we sewed   words,   spoke,
surrounded   by the selves   that could   have
spoken,   those   ghost   selves
that   lifted   from us   as we
turned   toward, as   we turned   away—
and   invisibly   became   all the
selves   we   never   became,
for   whatever   reason—

49

The Worms

The worms were tapping on my forehead.
They tapped with the blunt ends of their mouths.
They were testing the sturdiness of the ground.
They were testing the quality of the sediment.

Two worms crawled down my face to line
the lower edges of my cheek bones.
They drew a string they held between them.
A third worm plucked the string.
They were testing the pitch and tuning
of the gauntness of my face, of the tautness
of my skin across its scaffolding.
They were warming up the chorus and the soloists.

One worm shimmied under the string.
One worm hung its trousers on the string.
One worm balanced on the string holding a parasol.
One worm used the string to shoot an arrow up into the sky.

Shoot at the sun, shoot at the sun,
one worm bellowed into its megaphone.
One worm belted field positions.
One worm preached a sermon.
One worm placed a catalog order, artisanal handiworks.
One worm struck a hard rubber mallet on its metallophone.

Some worms listening to the sermon lay writhing on their sides.
Some shrieked like terrible children.

Some worms listening to the sermon lay draped limp over the dirt pews.
A worm listening to the metallophone tried to wedge his way
under the instrument, for an "intimate experience of the music."
A worm in the dirt manse embroidered crosses on a worm stole.

I was lying on my back in the fluorescent
nurse's room, a curtain drawn around my cot.
A worm-voice over the high school loudspeaker
interrupted the broadcast of my favorite
patriotic anthem. A crackle in its voice
made me long for dry cereal with profound
emptiness and irrational desire. The worm-voice said,
"Will Oni Buchanan please come
to the main office." "Oni Buchanan."
"Come to the main office." Go
to the main office, the school nurse
said to me.

17-Year Diagnosis

I photograph myself beneath
a street sign indicating
an evacuation route. I collect
dehydrated foods
for the emergency kit. I disperse
the remaining marigold seeds
over a plot of unlikely dirt. "I dare you!"
I shout to the distant officer.
Am I not meant to achieve
what others cannot?
I deprive myself

of an adequate serving.
I refuse all compensation.
I relinquish my significant lead.
I quietly close and put away
the dictionary and thesaurus.
I crouch under the giant bush
rubbing wet clay over my face.
Am I meant to medicate myself
down to a pincushion of vibrating needles?
My eyes peer out, guilty. I think back

on the hibernating ladybugs
cloistered inside the cement tower
rising from the abandoned hill.
Masses of faded red bodies

piled up on one another
like a mountain of pills waiting
to be shuttled into bottles, portioned out
in dosages, swallowed by a "patient," or,
that person with a desperate wish
to change, exchange
their molecules or un-derange—
"Patient," an electric humming
of collaborating complacencies.
And then when summer came,
over-ripened, the swarming cicadas

formed an inescapable
grid in the air. All the
buoyant, buzzing bodies. A pinball machine
of ideas, and the will
ricocheting from one elastic
possibility to the next, racking up
collision points before dropping exhausted
through an unseen
hole in the floor, trapdoor,
just one loose cranial plate
and a bottomless drop beneath. The un-medicated
beating of wings. They festered

over plants and trees and rocks. They crawled
unbidden from the ground with
implacable, unreadable eyes, red and
opaque, a hooked leg bent
into the bark. Am I only led

by the particular tint
of my vision? The sustained pulse
folding thicker to a shriek. Time-lapse
release. Husks of bodies
clawed onto the trees, each
back split open where a new,
whole life emerged. Is it so unfair to surge

ahead, with the speed built
into the body? An aberration, an
adaptation? Will you recognize me
by my face? The filmy carapace
just bursting at the seams? I'll beat
my new wet wings
against a fern.

Two-Starred Constellation

I'm not sure
so how am I supposed to say this
so how am I supposed to broach
this kind of topic

There is one subtracted, two subtracted
more, more, one at a time
until only a pill is left, a pill of
two people each half a capsule
holding dust inside them
holding ashes, mingling
dust and ashes
Everybody else is a bitch
Everybody else is such a little bitch

This two-starred
constellation just spinning around
its own center like a baton
enamored by its own glittering
tassels, shredded foil
twirling way up in the air

No, don't fill yourself
now, don't fix yourself
now, don't manage it, no
not now when you've
got it all worked out that bad

when you're raking it in
from having it all
worked out that bad

It's rotten at the core
The roots are rotten, hollow
and lined with fuzzy
rot, the flowers fell off
one by one, rot
streamlined to the nurturing
point, the leaves pulled off
like decayed teeth, fastened
to the stem by a rot thread

We watered the rot
More rotten We fertilized
the rot It multiplied
its rot The rot became too
extensive too
complicated to manage It
sinewed its way
into the interior
It marbled the interior
like a fatty ham

Give it to me
Give me what's mine
What's mine is mine
What I deserve
Give me my share

It's my turn now
What a disappointment
You've grown up to be
such a little bitch
Such a hateful little bitch
You're just like the rest
You're making me do this to you
You're making me do this

III.

Little Pig

That's right, Little Pig,
you're allowed to do anything you want.
That's right, Little Pig.
You're allowed.
Whatever you like, Little Pig,
you can do it today
while the sun is up,
while the cedar chips are warm,
while there are fresh grain pellets in your food dish.
It's time to choose from all the many things
you like to do, which one to do
first, which one to do second.
The day has begun for you,
Little Pig. It is a sunny day today,
indoors, but near the window—

*

Ring that little bell with your nose, Little Pig!
There's a bell there, and it's hanging down like that
so that you can ring it! Ring, ring, ring! It's time
for the world to know! There's a joyful noise
in the air, Little Pig, and you're
making it, you're streaming it through the air
like a beautiful red ribbon!

*

Those are some nice green leaves you've got,
Little Pig! Those are some nice green leaves
you've got there. Those green leaves have nice
curly edges; it's special to eat
leaves like that, Little Pig, those leaves with
a ruffle around the edge, thick green leaves, crisp
and wet, you look so happy
like you know
how special it is. I bet those are some
good-tasting leaves, Little Pig.

*

Sometimes it's nice to chew on cardboard,
Little Pig. A nice tube of cardboard, or the edges
of an oatmeal drum. It's nice if somebody
opens up both ends of the drum so you can
run through it, or nibble on the edges of the drum,
a tentative nibble before you
commit yourself to a whole-hearted
chewing, full absorption with your
industry of teeth, and your eyes just
looking out either side of your head like that,
just staring out not really at anything.
You can chew from inside the drum,
or from the outside, from
wherever you so happen
to be situated, Little Pig, to be able to chew
right from where you are is a nice
convenience these days.

*

Someone could build you a house
of soft pine wood, Little Pig. Because your teeth
are always growing
and somebody's got to keep them
manageable, Little Pig, they need to fit
in your own mouth and not
hurt you, your own teeth, Little Pig,
like a miniature monster
terrorizing you from inside your own
mouth. You could chew on the soft pine
of your house or on some cardboard tubes
or a little bit on your salt lick
if you can stand the taste for very long.
Chewing on newspaper isn't as fun. Too
inky and dirty, who wants to eat
all that dirt and all those
words. It's enough to make a Little Pig
sick with all that ink and horrible
meaning. You'd like to think
nobody aspires to keep
up-to-the-moment on the most
depraved human behavior, nobody
enjoys gawking at the latest inconceivable and
gruesome murder, nobody's a
voyeur in that way
of total indecency and complete disregard for other
living things. Shredded office paper is okay
but not as satisfying, pre-shredded like that,

in that prefabricated way. We all know
the teeth need to do their own
shredding, their own tearing
to wear themselves down—

*

Somebody could build your house
with both ends open
so you can run through your house
as free as a bird sweeping through the rafters,
as free as a prairie dog running through
short subterranean tunnels that open
onto dry, waving grasses, as free as
(slowed down in passing frames) a snake
molting from its old skin, emerging in renewed
colors, then living, molting
again, it's like a new
house every time you return!
And somebody could fit your house
with a jumping block jutting
perpendicularly from the outside wall,
you could run out one side
of the house and loop
around, leaping over the block before you
run back in the other side—
Perpetual joy is in that loop, Little Pig!
And in the leap, pure exhilaration
punctuating the joy, can it get
any better? Can we ask for more than that?

*

It's nice to see you so early this morning, Little Pig,
with your soft nose peeking in from the
running track doorway!
I see you've already
been exploring, maybe sniffing
with your soft nose in distant
corners of your pig environment.
It is good and wise to navigate one's world
with one's nose, as the dawn breaks
and the smells too crack open—
Did you find a fragrant surprise
fit for such a soft and delicate
muzzle? Did you find a wisp of scent,
fragile, delightful, a hint, a barely detectable
joy, a pleasure that you uncovered with your
devotion and your exploration?
Little Pig, you are the detective of joy.
You follow all the clues and find it
right where it is hidden.

*

It's a very nice and special thing
to be a Little Pig. There are so many
special sounds a pig can make,
including emphatic squealing, a low, vibrating
purring kind of sound, and then your median oink,
the general and continuous commentary

of contentedness throughout the day.
And a pig's excitement is so easily,
so fluently expressed, and free for all
to hear—"Something good is about
to happen!" "I know something good
is coming this way!" For there are many
deceptions that will make a Little Pig
misperceive—or—hope for the best, because
a Little Pig is your permanent optimist.
Be it the sound of a plastic bag crinkling
or house keys jangling or the refrigerator door
opening—a Little Pig will always jump
to the best possible conclusion, the best
possible outcome, and a Little Pig's full faith
in these ambiguous situations is
a true joy to behold. It is often
that a Little Pig crafts her own
destiny by so moving anyone who listens
to provide for her the joy that she expects,
a piece of lettuce, a grape or carrot, a slice of
berry, a scratch behind the ears, for any
of these things will please a Little Pig beyond
earthly measure, shame, shame on us.

*

It's okay to run on your track, Little Pig.
Run around as fast as you can.
Listen to that scuffle your tiny claws
make on the plywood track!

You can go faster than you ever thought
possible, you are a streak of rainbow,
you are a shooting star, Little Pig! Do you know
what that is, have you ever seen
the night, I mean, the night that has stars
and not just darkness, not just a
carpeted black? Listen to your speed, Little Pig!
You can run as fast as you want!
It will all be fine if you run and run,
you can run all day! You can run all night!
You can run until you're tired! You can jump too,
just a little leaping as you run, just a leap
into the air now and then as you run,
you can feel your whole
body in the air—you're free, Little Pig!
You're free from the ground!

*

And you are such a nimble pig, even though
you are shaped a bit like a
stuffed Christmas stocking
or a somewhat bulky burrito
or a hoagie with too many
toppings or a woolly-bear caterpillar, you are built
somehow to run and leap and find joy
in the air, I hear you
oinking as you run, for joy! Not every animal
sings as it runs and that makes you
special, a special creature, Little Pig.

A Little Pig is what we should
aspire to be in our own dull and compromised
minds, our calloused, sickly,
unseemly minds, fetid in a bath of bile.
Our degraded, offcast,
baseless, contemptible, vulgar,
sordid minds. Our minds, marinating
in peevishness and overloaded with the latest
tally of wrongs committed against our own
pristine unaccountability. Dishonorable and indelicate,
Little Pig, we are not fit
to take care of you, and so often
we fail and you do not get to live
like you deserve through no
fault of your own, Little Pig, through no
failing of your own. No failing of your
character, no failing of your instinct, no
failing of your efforts. It's not because you didn't
try your very best.

*

Shake that water bottle, Little Pig.
Shake the gosh darn heck out of that empty
water bottle. Because everyone should know
that pigs need water to slake their thirst,
that all pigs need a little water because their
mouths get a little bit dry, that's what
happens when you're alive, it's only the
natural thing, and a Little Pig needs some water

to keep going through the day. Thrash
the heck out of that plastic bottle, Little Pig.
Everyone needs to know that they need
to provide you with enough
water for your thirst, Little Pig. Water
for your present thirst and water for your future thirst.
And some water to dribble from the sides
of your mouth as you drink.
Because everyone knows that a water bottle
is not the most efficient dispenser
of water, but you catch what you can,
Little Pig. You drink water as best as you can,
until you don't feel thirsty anymore, until
the moment of your thirst has passed and you don't
notice it anymore, you can
forget about it for the time being without even
trying, your attention moves to a new
place, easy and unconcerned—

*

It's nice to reach up into the hay feeder
to pull down some nice fresh hay or timothy
with your teeth,
some clean, dry hay that smells fresh and nice
and tastes good too.
It's nice to eat hay in the afternoon
when a fresh batch arrives in the feeder.
"Somebody that loves me
put that hay there," you can think as you chew.

It's almost like the sun
warmed that hay for you,
like the sun is feeding you
with an outstretched and friendly ray.

*

Good job, Little Pig, you did such a
good job today eating all the
food pellets out of your food dish, I heard you
crunching on some pellets, they're like
chewable vitamins, lots of
good, healthy things in those there
pellets and you did a good job eating
every last one, cleaning out your whole
food dish, you didn't even throw a tantrum
and flip your entire food dish
upside-down and urinate on its contents
or somehow accidentally get a poop
mixed in with the pellets, it's a good thing
not to get poops in your food dish, those are
some nice manners you've got,
Little Pig, a real regal sense of
etiquette, you could have guests
over, you could author a manual, you could
receive foil-backed invitations
and purchase doilies, soon you'll be eating
with the King and Queen at Buckingham
Palace, soon I'll be saying that I knew you
way back when—

*

Hello, good morning! You are a very nice
and alert pig! Good morning, nice pig! I must say,
you're looking a little bit fat today, Little Pig,
your rear is looking awfully
big, no offense,
like maybe you ate too much for
a few weeks in a row, maybe you
dreamed too much there, lounging on those
wood chips or in your little house, maybe
you chewed on some food in your sleep,
because today it's catching up to you,
Little Pig, you look a bit plump, maybe a little bit
fat and ungainly, maybe it would be easier
on you if you just lost a little bit
around the middle, kept it slim, Little Pig.

*

Today we can go outside, Little Pig!
I'm home and I'm going to play with you,
it's sunny today and the grass
is long! I found some dandelions
growing in the yard, you can sit
beneath the yellow soft explosion
like your own personal sun
and chew on the jagged bitter greens
you somehow find delicious— Maybe
it is true that every bitter thing you touch

becomes infused with a sweetness it thought
was long lost, a sweetness it thought
was no longer available to it, not now, not
after all these years, all this
time and harshness.

*

You are made to be such a nice creature,
Little Pig, you are a blessing to be around
for anyone. For all people.
It is an honor to be near you, Little Pig.
It is an honor to be recognized by you
as your friend. I passed a local church recently,
and its marquee announced there would be
a "Blessing of the Animals" that particular
weekend. I thought, how can it *possibly* be
that we disgusting, selfish, devouring
humans, avaricious and insatiate, rapacious
and inconsolable, filled with soiled rags
and gasoline and crumpled dollar bills,
filled with attics of rusty fans and quarry-depths
of submerged machinery, invisible blades
that dismember eager and shivering swimmers, filled
with trash compactors and glutted
disposals clogged with peels, amalgamated
monstrosities, how can it be
that we could deign to offer our
"Blessing of the Animals" to a population
ravaged by our greed, we like a plague

destroying them as we breed
and spread like a clutching, limitless disease?
We are a godawful
species, Little Pig, obstinate
and useless. Yet you animals offer us a
blessing every day that we observe you, every
hour that we spend with you, every minute
that we think of you, you animals
offer us a blessing but nobody
hears it because guess why.
Nobody is listening. Not here, Little Pig.
The ears are stopped with clay.

*

It's okay to take a nap, Little Pig.
It's okay to take a little nap
in the middle of the afternoon when you might
be tired, Little Pig, or if it's
too hot out, it's okay
to take a nap if you need to lie down
or rest, if you feel a little bit sleepy
and the cedar chips seem restful, if it seems
comforting to lie down a little bit
or to stretch out, it's okay, Little Pig.
You can lie in the sun or in the shade
as you like. You can lie in the open
or in your little house if you need
some privacy or if you want to dream,
if there's something more, you can dream

about what's outside, about another
world, Little Pig, where the grass grows high
and you can eat in the sun whenever
you like, and other little
pigs like you nearby eating grass—

*

Little Pig, you are a special, special creature,
and if everybody doesn't know it, if they're
more worried about their designer manicures and their
subwoofers and their vanity plates and their
gym memberships and their pant suits, that's not
your problem. You just keep right on doing
what you like best. Something will come of it
as the days pass and pass, or maybe
not. Maybe nothing will come of it.
Because nobody knows if a joy
will be waiting at the end of all their
efforts. But you, you
could care less, since you find
a hidden joy in all things. You
are the sweetest creature
there ever was. How were you
made and how do you
bring joy to everyone who meets you,
no matter what, no matter who? You are the common
denominator, Little Pig, it's only you.

*

Good night, sweet pig, good night.
It's nice to give you one last pat
before we both go to sleep for the night.
You can go into your remotest
hidey-hole and curl up
in the darkest corner if that's
what you like. All pigs need a place
that is all their own, where nobody
can reach in and drag them out.
All pigs deserve to be completely
inaccessible when it's important to them
to have a little privacy. Because all pigs deserve
to have their private lives and their own
dignity. Even though it's fun to think
that we both go to sleep together,
I know that actually the night
is one of your favorite times
to do whatever you do, Little Pig,
because sometimes I wake up and I hear you
making your soft gentle noises
or running as fast as you can.
You have your own projects, Little Pig,
that I am not privy to, that I will never
understand and I love you
for that, for your entirely
private and personal undertakings.
Thank you for humoring me, for greeting me
with a kind and happy look, an eager
and welcoming look, in the morning when I

rejoin the world and find you
joyful and excited to see me. It's nice
to wake up to you, Little Pig.
It's nice to aspire to be
deserving of your love, the love
of one Little Pig, unique in all the world.

IV.

Must a Violence

Must a violence be administered
Must a violence be enacted upon
Must a violence be had to oneself
Must a violence be endured
Must an unanticipated violence
Must a violence beyond one's control
Must a modicum of violence
Must a dosage or capsule-full of violence
Must an irregularly dispensed occasional
vaccination of violence
Must a violence be inflicted upon
Must a violence first be undergone

Unless a machine is built
Unless a machine can anticipate
Unless a machine's precision
Unless the exactitude of a machine can be employed
Unless the clean functionality of a machine
Unless the useful reliability of a machine
Unless a machine's metallic composition
Unless a machine's efficiency and preoccupation
Unless the spinning cogs of a well-oiled machine
Unless the gears and circuitry of a handsome machine
Unless a machine whose constant vibrating hum
Unless a machine in synchronization
Unless a threshing machine be devised
Unless a winnowing machine

Unless a machine is invented by inventors
Unless a machine can first predict
Unless a machine can graph and then extrapolate

How many hits does it take
How many hits to disassemble
How many hits to scatter the ingredients in a useful circumference
How many hits to de-contextualize
How many hits to see the material
on its own terms
How many hits to purify the elements
How many hits to distill the proper essence
How many hits to extract the volatile components
How many hits not to ask what your country
can do for you
How many hits to jar the assumptions just enough
How many hits to isolate the isotopes
How many hits to hammer at white heat
How many hits to break the bonds and re-forge
the remnant molecules
How many hits to loosen like a tooth
that offers a newer tooth beneath
How many hits to solve a logic puzzle
by ejection button
How many hits to tear the canvas and break the glass
How many hits to lay it all out
How many hits are just enough hits
How many hits are not one too many hits
How many hits are the perfect number of hits
How many hits are the exact duress of hits

How many hits to achieve a boiling point of matter
How many hits to execute with great precision
How many hits to reach a certain brink

What is the certainty of the brink
What is the indisputable defining
characteristic of the brink
What is the *je ne sais quoi* of the brink
What is the elusive, unplaceable perfume
worn discreetly at the brink
What is the quality of air surrounding the brink
What is the punctured skin or surface area of the brink
What is the ragged groundwork, the contour of the brink
What is the fluctuating elevation of the brink
What is the mercurial temperature by day
and by night of the brink
What is the precise longitude and latitude of the brink
What are the geological constituents of the brink
What is the constitutional makeup of the brink
Is there a flag staked at the brink
Is there my country's flag staked at the brink
Is my family's crest staked at the brink
Is my clan's necessary plaid staked at the brink
Is there a base camp at the brink
Is there a campfire at the brink
Is there room for footwork at the brink
Is there a showcase at the brink
Is there a rationing of provisions at the brink
Are the comestibles divided fairly at the brink
Will the pork be salted at the brink

Is the brink made of salt
Is the brink made of ice
Is the brink made of stone
Is the brink made of red clay
Is the brink made of dust
Is the brink made of petrified wood
Is the brink made of flower stems
Is the brink made of animal pelts
Is the brink made of egg shells
Is the brink made of fruit rinds
Is the brink made of rats' nests
Is the brink made of calcite
Is the brink made of teeth
Is the brink made of feathers
Is the brink made of straw
Is the brink made of chaff

Everybody

Well it started when I wondered
if I had something to say
and I did not. So much
work needs to get done anyway.
Some songs need to be
photocopied for the routine
and we need to think up
some skits involving grass skirts.
High tide is coming in
and the gulls are being aggressive
as usual. One child uselessly
digs a ditch which keeps filling
with water. The sky
is clear and blue with one big
streak of cloud across it like a vacant
sash. The waves
come in ringing. It's a high
frequency. Algae pulses
in the water like bile thrown up
from the gut of the ocean. It doesn't matter
anyway. It's a question
of perception, all these strangers
in the water. All our misshapen
bodies telling their own unspoken
mythologies. Everyone wants
to get in the water

below the blue sky below the
blaring sun. The rhythm rolls in
again and again. I had enumerated
the party ideas in a tidy list
that I communicated to others involved
who will convene tonight to discuss
the array of activities. A vote
will be conducted and specific
festivity contributions will be
assigned to specific individuals.
A helicopter flies by and everyone's
attention is drawn upward. However impossible
it all may be, objectivity. Sometimes a person
finally overhears himself,
the voice that had been going on all the while.
The sand has gotten all over my towel
and the black flies bother me with their
tiny relentless biting. Families
kick by in the sand, hauling coolers
and colorful umbrellas.
The beach is clearing out
here in the late afternoon and soon
I will be eating a food item
and dreaming up party favors.
Everybody just creating
endless tedious obligations
for one another. "Because it's
my turn. It's my turn now."
A girl drags her yellow bucket

through the water and comes back
to fill the castle moat.
An electric fence is erected around
a part of the beach right in our midst
where the piping plovers are nesting.
Because only an actual electric fence
on the public beach will keep us
from trampling down a limited group
of fragile plovers
in order to get pictures of the plovers
or see the plovers better or see
what everybody else is jostling to see.

Attention Span

A cupcake will not solve this.
A shared ice cream treat
with hot fudge will not

solve it. Things are accidentally
spilled, toppled, my contempt
grows. Finish one motion

before you begin the next.
Have an attention span
that brings you to the

end point of an endeavor.
Solve a problem and
incorporate the solution

into your daily lifestyle
until it becomes habit.
It's not "natural," I know,

but is learning "natural"?
Is choosing to do a
difficult thing "natural"?

I see you're looking forward
to the next time the trough
will be filled with slop

and not much further
forward than that. One
slop bucket to the next,

potato peels and runoff.
Oh feast table
of the wealthy innovators

and seers, successful
entrepreneurs, could you give us
a lesson that will stick?

Could you teach us
a hard lesson? The same dog
comes and the same dog goes,

running, sometimes holding a Frisbee
in its mouth. The babies
expand in number.

The din of babies interrupts
the atmosphere. Their strollers
take up the thoroughfare, pushing

the rest of us into the road, into
the bike lane, oncoming
traffic. There's a skunk

on the road too.
It gets flatter and flatter
each day, ground in with the

tarred-down macadam,
into the finite cracks. Even its
singular defense, its stink,

is dissipating in the air
as the body lingers.
Soon it will somehow

be gone, absorbed
into the mundane pores
of the surrounding materials.

The Occupation

You see, it really is a lot of work
because there is a lot of mud, you see,

especially when it rains so much
like it has and makes mud

upon mud, mud all the way
down, and then it really becomes

quite the occupation to
move all that mud

from one side to the other,
to push all that mud back and forth, to sort

one mud from another mud.
I was an industrious pig.

In my pen I pushed a ball of mud
from one end to the other—

There is so much mud to distribute
and so much works against my

perfect placement of mud,
against all my efforts. It rains and

my piles of mud are destroyed, are rendered
sloppy, festering pools

where loathsome mosquitos breed. At least
I can wallow, but to make progress,

to make any progress at all,
one needs a certain

substance to the mud, a certain texture, a
structural integrity

to the mud to build on it,
to build mud upon mud—

I suppose I am all design, all strategy and design.
All lofty, ephemeral dreaming,

enchantment and charm, unlikeliness—
The sun as a kiln could work for me

if the sun worked at all.
There is no moderation on this earth.

Or maybe that's just it.
Maybe there is only moderation.

Jury Duty

But of course the limits
of our perception are so severe.
I just don't understand

how I'm supposed to sit
for jury duty and that somehow
it's my duty as a flawed citizen

to produce flawed judgments.
Because you can't know
anyone and you can't

trust anyone, let alone yourself.
Everyone has their own
motives and half the time

they don't understand them
and that's why we're all
in court in the first place.

My blood is louder
under low concrete bridges,
in close passageways,

in culverts in the hillside—
the fact is fairly obvious.
I can go underneath the hill

on my hands and knees!
I can hide in the woods!
"Remember when you used

to run away to the woods?"
I hope I never have to be
the object of legal judgments

passed by a panel of people
who don't question their ability
to pass judgments. But mother, mother,

help me calculate my income taxes. I've got
all the categories worked out
and my QuickBooks file is entirely

up-to-date. I'm talking to-the-minute
accuracy. Because I'm more organized
than humanly possible.

I'm superhumanly organized.

This Here Minute

"Don't make me
choose between you," she said

from the recesses
of her heavy fabric curtain. I heard her

flip an egg timer to measure
the minutes of this portion

of my punishment, or "the minutes"
subdivided into falling

grains of sand— Let's get it
moving, people. Let's get it

done already. Let's take care of this
monkey business. I listened

to the air I breathed,
the same air that held the hourglass.

The sound was always in the process of
going one way or the other. I listened

through the magnetic fluctuation
of the glass to hear inside it,

sand grains falling
within that inner

air. "Less than a minute
left," I heard her sob. Let's see

just how much we can get done
in this here minute. Let's get

on with it. None
is less than a little bit.

Fly away, balloons!
Fly away, festooned with all your ashes!

Mechanics

Oh life which I hate
Oh wading pool of dirt and runoff
Oh tree chipper roaring and chewing and spitting out again
Oh curly, curly pig tail sprightly on the pig bottom
Oh shirtless, overweight retiree
punctuating talk radio
with deep personal belches
Squelched talents like shriveled walnuts
rattling in the shell, the tensed muscles
You can see I am over-obligated
I have chosen a difficult profession
Though I kept my nose to the grindstone
Though I kept my ear to the ground
Though I put my shoulder to the wheel
Still it appears
I have over-committed myself
to the needs of others, to offering solutions
to the selfish, blunt-headed needs
of others, to the litigious, masturbatory
prick-waving of others
Must it be so, Lord?
What a tricksy gamer who builds things
with blobs of oil
What a tricksy gamer who sells old clothing items
to purchase new clothing items
What a tricksy gamer who responds to job advertisements

with links to other job advertisements
No really, I am full of awe
Hit me with a hammer, Lord
Hit me with a chisel made of crystal glass
But don't let him die
Don't let him die yet
How could it be
the mechanics of this day, this hour,
hide a better, more perfect
mechanics?

Sometimes a Body

It's hard to see things differently
without the person
without the voice of the person, but

more, the body that holds the voice,
the body that moves from one side
of the room to the other.

Someone insistent on arguing
can see aging on the body.
Can see weakness. The voice

comes from the weakness
of the body. It shows a different
angle. It reveals alternative

possibilities. Compassion comes
from watching the gestures
of a body. Without the person there

it's hard to re-imagine. It's hard
to see another way. Sometimes
a body there is a necessary

intervention. It shows someone
obstinate with righteousness
where a voice is coming from.

Do you see where I'm coming from?
And the vulnerability of the body
measures the content of the words

of the voice. The body's vulnerability
tempers the temper of the words
of the voice, it opens up a new

brilliant corridor filled with
light. Some may think it's
divine light that touches and

illuminates another possibility.
But it's more than that. It's a light
that shines through

tears that hang from the golden
corridor ceiling on nylon fishing line.
The tears on their lines are fastened

to the ceiling with transparent
thumbtacks. The light shines through
all the tears, refracting pendants

of unspeakable pain, and this is what
makes the shimmering and causes
the image to shift. The movement

makes compassion in the light; it's like
a piece moves in the skull. A fused piece
shifts like an effortless opening door—

Has His Smell and Taste

Has his smell changed in any way or become offensive to you

      No I love his smell, he smells the same

Are you still in love with how he smells and how he tastes

      Yes I love his smell and taste

Does he smell like you remember

      He has the most wonderful smell I'm not sure how it is

Does he taste the same

      Yes, always, he always tastes good to me

But does he taste the way he always has

      Better, his taste improves and grows more sweet with time

Would you describe his taste in terms of the natural world

      Like honeysuckle, honeydew melon,

      like gentle clover, like a snowy expanse of field in the sunshine,

      like the smell of cold

Is it a world you love or has your love changed

Like folded handmade paper, like a bicycle path by the ocean

I said your love, has it changed, has your love changed for the world you inhabit

Always a music, the songs materialize from thin air,

the sounds emanate from the raw materials, radiant

But has your love grown old for the world

We move through tall gorgeous chords inside which

melodies flicker and attract

Has the world grown slow for your love

We can lie down on a breath, there is warm sleep

in the silences, cotton and down, a loft of hay

Has its plumage faded, is the world a small brown bird in a thicket of sticks

A heart in its ribcage, a lighthouse beacon,

a generating electricity, a somersault, a high wire

Then is his taste fading as your love fades

Not fading no my love is tethered,

we share a pistachio cake with chocolate chips

So will you lose your love once that taste is gone

The cormorants are sunning their wings again on the log,

the family of turtles

So that smell is fading as your love fades

We take detours in the story, we find

the silhouettes of rabbits

So that love is fading as your lives fade

The wind is out again, anonymous chimes sound, we watch

the colors of the sky changing, we smell the burning

of leaves, we count the hunched bodies

of wild turkeys in the bare trees, the ground

is covered in snow, we push through the drifts

with chain treads tied to the bottoms of our boots

So the world is fading as your love fades?

V.

The Wild Rabbit

They froze hard, stared at one another from the sides of their heads—the wild rabbit, muscular on his haunches, and Sergei, soft, fluffy and plump, bred a jet black not of the natural world. Who can know what thoughts or recognitions, what early memories, what collective images of a lineage of species passed between them? The wild rabbit bolted away.

"Sergei, that was a wild rabbit, did you see that rabbit? A rabbit just like you!" I exclaimed. "Sergei, let's catch up with that rabbit!" I cried out, my voice tense and shrill. I ran a few steps and looked back over my shoulder, hoping Sergei would hop after me, hesitant at first perhaps, but then faster, more confident, growing into the stride, and then we would streak together through the far field like the wild rabbit had.

And then I hoped—I knew—Sergei would outstrip me, far outstrip me, flying on his powerful rabbit haunches, leaping, soaring over the field in bounds and zigzags, breathless with his own incredible strength and speed, his rabbit agility unleashed there at the brink of the crepuscular world, a rabbit's world, and he, suddenly one with his own mastery, his birthright, his ease—

And then I imagined—I hoped—Sergei would come back to me, find me on the periphery of his world at that spot where his bright existence outstreaked mine, fantastic as a passing comet. And he would forgive me then, and we could go home together in the dusk, back to my halogen-lamp-lit, lo-pile carpeted one-bedroom rental, rattling like a rotten tooth by the cargo tracks at the end of our dead-end street.

Outsource the Burning

Here they come again—yes they're stopping
to inhale—here they are at the bushes,
shaking the branch first

to scare the bees away
before they dip their faces
into the flowers.

Even the most deserted bodies
are in line for a service,
a costly service.

Something got out of whack
and now the rest of the machine
is swollen. A mixing

of ash from the fuel
with ash from the body— It's wheezing
with the effort, sore

in the joints and ligaments.
Is there a hole; is there
some dirt that could

expand to accept
the spill of words, absorb,
then dry out like a powder?

There's a river that snakes
through the land, bent back double
on itself, approaching with such oblique

folds and gestures, genuflections—
A filtration to separate dust particles
from dust-laden gases.

How does one evaluate
the "help" one has received?
But if the dirt gave up words

like an excess moisture and kept its
dry self, invisible wet havoc
soaked up into sky—

If drawn into the atmosphere,
if held in a matrix of cloud—
(Animals, don't turn your faces

upwards toward the sun; animals,
bend your muzzles low
to the long grass; bend down

to catch the scent of the river—)
And the water table absorbs,
the rhizomes

infiltrate, the black wet leaves
unfurl—the putrid flower catches
the passing legs of a worker bee—

Otherworldly Thirst

The rats are out drinking
at the edges of puddles.
Their thirst is unquenchable.
They wash their bodies clean
on the inside. They restore
order to their bodies.
Not tonight.
I'm not going to get poisoned tonight.
Trust the intense
desire of the body. Sharpen
it. Focus it
into an incinerating beam.
This hurricane is
rather pleasant. I find myself
enjoying this hurricane.
Is there anything I can do to help?
Yes, get yourself in order.
In fact, yes, pull yourself together.
Know thyself, as somebody once said.
Knit thyself together, tighten the
loose strands of ligament.
The rats are washing the poison
out of their systems
with huge gulpings.
The poison makes their bodies
extremely thirsty, gives

their bodies the clue to the only
thing that will save them.
Otherworldly thirst matched by
a standing puddle of water.
Water in left-out flower pots.
Gutter full of water.

This World

The sailboats are out on the river.
The colors are out; all the leaves are out;
the blue sky, cold and clear.

There's an amphibious vehicle
driving from the land straight
into the river—the people aboard

are all cheering. As for us, we're
driving to the ocean today, the edge
of the whole continent.

When we arrive, it's high tide
and the island a little ways out
from the shore rises from the choppy

surface of the water. The land bridge
is underwater, and I can only imagine
the starfish are marching across

for an afternoon in the tide pools.
On the beach, a lone teenager
is trying to fly his kite. He's old enough

to have made the choice to bike here,
just himself and his kite and his
determination to buoy it in the air.

At a distance away, a man
practices with his sword, stark
movements on the sand, a discipline

of exact movement, exact stillness
and repetition. There is a house
poised at the edge of the ocean.

On the very top floor is a single
square room with one window
on each side, a crow's nest

looking out over the rocks
where the water breaks, where
the crabs gather. Damp channels

are left carved in the sand as the tide
pulls out again. A dog sits down
in the low waters and lets his squeaky toy

get pulled in and returned to him
again and again by the waves,
following it with his gaze, just watching—

See

Six or seven yards behind you in the city smog
a man carrying a dog like a toddler
(its front paws around his neck)
calls your name, or what could only

be your name, he's looking straight
at you as you stare absently
at something else across this noisy street.
The dog looks into the face of the man

then looks where the man's eyes
are looking—straight at you—you
have not yet realized you're part
of this scene though there's

your body standing quiet
on the public sidewalk. The dog
is so sincere. The man is walking
toward you. He's carrying

the little brown dog
with the tight matted curls. He calls
your name again. Theresa, I know
what's about to happen—you're about

to recognize his voice,
you're about to pull his voice like
a lavender ribbon from the gray blur
of other noises in the air, and then

the syllables will focus, your name
will cohere out of the ether and
be yours like the worn cloth carnation
pinned to your slightly crumpled

coat lapel. You'll turn around, toward
his voice, toward your name. The dog
will look at you, earnest and slightly
worried, eager to please. You already

know these lives. You're about to
hear, you're about to turn, you hear, you
turn, now what do you
see that I can't see

from right here on the sidewalk, me,
invisible as the parked cars, the row
of metal mailboxes, this single gum-stuck
lamppost? What do you see?

I Was a Whale

I was a whale extending a flipper
I rolled over and over to feel the water
coursing over my powerful body
I am so immense unstoppable and yet
the water surrounds me and
holds me up I am not made
of machinery I am pure
light coursing through a tube
Oh voice of my father
Oh voice of my teacher
They call to me underwater I turn my belly to the sun

I was a complicated instrument
I had silver valves and alternating pistons
curving brass slides that could be removed and put back again
I carved my own mouthpiece
from a waving reed cut down at the water's edge
The length of a breath was the length
of a bow drawn across me
The strings hummed The sun
gleamed off my metals
Oh velvet revolt of sound into the cold, cracked air
Oh changing tones reflecting the
roundness of the mouth the density of thought

I was an inchworm hanging from a silken thread
Invisible I was a living

green digit counting in units of one
each guilty body as it passed oblivious
I chastised the striding arm
I measured the error
over the skin's expanse
I matched the dirty exhale with a fluctuating air
My purity canceled out the trespass
and left a vacuum where I fell
and gained a footing on the mottled earth
Oh generosity withheld
Oh unspoken apology

I was an audience a congregation I
was a lobotomy ward I was single-minded
in my endeavor
the wasp hovering just above
I was a sled of regrets
dragged over gravel
I was furiously weaving at the
structural lines Oh threadbare life-forms
Oh lungs that pump the sour air
I was a fog machine
beneath a heavy broad rock

I was an invisible wheel in my own heart
turning, turning as the rest of me
rode my bicycle down the street
I was the toothed mechanism
ground flat I was
the somewhat deflated lining

A glass shard hurt
from an undetectable location
I was tainted with a compromised oil I
sought traction as the beatings
surrounded me in the pitch
I can't tell if it's me
or the machinery to which I am
affixed Tiredness
radiates from the exact
center Oh fuse
Heart of the
invisible wheel of the heart

Younger and Younger

The clouds are stuck in the tops of trees
down there on the mountain.

They make it look like a fire
burning at the root of the forest,
a ground fire, somehow,
spreading in lines that leave smoke
rising to the sky.

Or like gauze stuffed into
the wounds of the mountain,
stitched power line paths cut in,
trees bleeding from the woodpeckers'
ambition.

Or like thoughts teased out from the murmur
of trees, misty at the edges, ready to
disperse altogether,
or form and rise up
into the sky—a floating fever,
a halo of thought, radioactive scribblings—

The clouds tug at the trees
from above. White insistent molecules,
pulling the trees
into blue molecules of sky.
The clouds tug at the sky

from below. The breath of the skies,
pulled into dense green forest needles.
I'm flying backwards
through the day, getting three hours younger.
Younger and younger. The time I gain
tugs from above. I will trade in
three hours of crying for three new hours:
blue sky, sunshine, and a park
overflowing with flowers.

The Sun Turns Like a Pinwheel

A raft stretches behind our mother
and we are on it, tethered to her strokes.

The sun turns like a pinwheel.
We saw it from our network

like a curving, fluctuating plane
of many dots. We spread out

like a blanket to keep the nightmares
unfiltered into air. Brutal

consolations. A uniform scathing;
some sizzle to leave behind

the body to its next breath-inhabitant
(a silver pass, invisible by day)— To plant

the vacant marrow, a raft.
We blister, we agonize in time,

a metrical occasion of days.
Night provides the bar line, the pause

between movements. Watery boulevard
of interference, indifference, a

no-man's land—char
across the landscape—

The sun turns like a pinwheel.
We gather inside it with our

armored shoulders all together,
clustered in the center. We are on

its platform. We are on the raft,
dragged along behind. We will be raised

toward it. Sometimes we grip
as hard as we can—the wind

would shake us from our
shimmering mission to receive

and to deflect again the scalding rays,
for its luminance makes

our luminance shine—
Our huddled bodies make a

compound eye—
A jeweled hint of emerald warning,

a scabbard leading to a dagger.
The sun turns like a pinwheel. It counts

its radiant, radioactive petals, ending always
in "love," an odd number—

ACKNOWLEDGMENTS

Sincere thanks to the editors of the following journals, in which poems from this book first appeared (with special thanks to Katie Ford at *New Orleans Review* and Nate Pritts at *H_NGM_N* for publishing features of my work):

Augury Books ("The Occupation"); *Boston Review* ("When All the Leaves"); *Catch Up* ("Attention Span"); *Clade Song* ("Little Pig"); *Columbia Poetry Review* ("Selection" and "The Wild Rabbit"); *Conduit* ("Five Tiny Doves" and "This World"); *Fence* ("Has His Smell and Taste" and "If You Love an Animal"); *H_NGM_N Poetry Journal* ("I Was a Whale," "Mechanics," "17-Year Diagnosis," "Sometimes a Body," and "Everybody"); *The Laurel Review* ("The Sun Turns Like a Pinwheel"); *Nevermore* ("Two-Starred Constellation"); *New Orleans Review* ("No Blue Morpho," "The Worms," "See," "Then From Our Green Branch," and "Must a Violence").

Enormous gratitude to Mark Levine for his fantastic, scrupulous editing work and revision suggestions.

And deepest thanks and love to Jon Woodward, without whom this book could not have been written.

KUHL HOUSE POETS

Oni Buchanan
Must a Violence

Michele Glazer
On Tact, & the Made Up World

David Micah Greenberg
Planned Solstice

John Isles
Ark

John Isles
Inverse Sky

Bin Ramke
Airs, Waters, Places

Bin Ramke
Matter

Michelle Robinson
The Life of a Hunter

Robyn Schiff
Revolver

Robyn Schiff
Worth

Rod Smith
Deed

Cole Swensen
The Book of a Hundred Hands

Cole Swensen
Such Rich Hour

Tony Tost
Complex Sleep

Susan Wheeler
Meme

Emily Wilson
The Keep